Original title:
Yonder Threads Inside the Phoenix Dunk

Copyright © 2025 Swan Charm
All rights reserved.

Author: Lan Donne
ISBN HARDBACK: 978-1-80563-215-3
ISBN PAPERBACK: 978-1-80564-736-2

## Whirls of the Celestial Flame

In the silence of the night, they dance,
Flickering sparks in a cosmic trance.
Whirls of colors, deep and bright,
Casting shadows, chasing light.

Stars above, like watchful eyes,
Guide the dreams that softly rise.
Whispers carried on the breeze,
Secrets shared with midnight trees.

A fire's glow, a beacon's call,
In the dark, we feel it all.
Each flutter brings a tale untold,
In the warmth, we brave the cold.

Through the mists of time we weave,
Wonders born from those who believe.
With every flicker, hearts entwine,
In this dance of flame divine.

So let us twirl with joyful grace,
In the whirls of this sacred space.
Where magic lingers, dreams take flight,
A tapestry of stars ignites.

## Interweaving Stories of Flight

In realms where dreams take flight,
The whispers dance on gossamer night.
Feathers brush against the stars,
Tales are spun from distant bazars.

Through clouded paths, the heart's delight,
Unfolds in hues of silver light.
Each soul a story, brightly sewn,
In skies where secrets freely roam.

### Firelit Reflections

Beneath the glow of fiery flames,
Shadows twirl and whisper names.
A flicker holds the past's embrace,
In every glint, a frozen trace.

The embers speak of tales untold,
Of bravery, both fierce and bold.
Mirrored dreams on parchment reside,
In warmth where whispered thoughts confide.

## The Aria of Rising Wings

Awake! The dawn, a choir sings,
As velvet skies hold rising wings.
With every note, the world ignites,
In melodies of soaring heights.

Here, silence bows to vibrant sound,
In echoes where our hearts are found.
The symphony of hope takes flight,
In harmonies that chase the night.

## Ascent Through the Fiery Veil

Through swirling flames, the journey starts,
Where courage mounts, and fear departs.
With every breath, the fire grows,
A dance of fate, where magic flows.

The veil of dusk, a canvas bright,
In shades of red and amber light.
We ascend beyond the earthly ties,
As dreams unfold beneath the skies.

## Chronicles of Fiery Wings

In the realm where dragons soar,
A tale of hearts forever more.
With each flap, the flames ignite,
A dance of shadows in the night.

Through whispers soft the legends pass,
Of courage found within the glass.
With fiery wings, the dreams take flight,
To carve the sky, igniting light.

## Tapestry of Renewal

Beneath the stars, the loom does weave,
Threads of hope that sparkle and cleave.
Each moment stitched with care, alive,
In every fiber, dreams will thrive.

The weary ground begins to heal,
Nature's rhythm starts to reveal.
As blossoms burst from darkened soil,
Life awakens, tender and loyal.

## **The Heartbeat of Resilience**

In shadows deep, the heart beats strong,
Through trials faced, where we belong.
Like rivers flowing, fierce and clear,
Resilience blooms, casting out fear.

When storms arise and tempests roar,
We gather strength, we seek for more.
Each heartbeat whispers, never yield,
For in our souls, the light is sealed.

## Ashes Weaving Tomorrow's Story

From ashes cold, new dreams emerge,
A phoenix rising, with a surge.
In every ember, a tale unfolds,
Of battles fought and courage bold.

With every dawn, the past dissolves,
In whispered winds, the future solves.
We craft anew from what was lost,
A quilt of colors, no matter the cost.

## Weaving Within the Singed Memory

In shadows deep, old whispers call,
Threads of time in the starlit sprawl.
Ink and ember, tales entwined,
Memories dance, in silence confined.

Through the haze, a flicker bright,
Lost in the tapestry of night.
Woven dreams, sharp and clear,
In the golden glow, hold them dear.

Faded echoes, a lullaby's hum,
Loom of fate, where shadows come.
Stitched in silence, they weave and sway,
In the heart's corner, forever they'll stay.

Frayed edges, yet strong the seam,
Binding the past with a fervent dream.
In the fire's heart, the stories renew,
In the singed memory, whispers are true.

## **Artisan of Burning Dreams**

With hands of flame and heart of gold,
An artisan crafts the dreams untold.
Each spark a wish, each blaze a thought,
From the glowing forge, creation is wrought.

Through the night, the embers gleam,
As hopes take flight like a soaring beam.
Melding desire with the fire's breath,
From ashes born, a dance with death.

Through twisted oak and strands of light,
He casts a web, both fierce and bright.
In stolen moments, the flames abide,
While fragile hearts in ember can ride.

The winds of change, they whip and twine,
A tapestry sewn with threads divine.
In the furnace of life, the sparks ignite,
Artisan's dreams reach astonishing height.

## The Fragile Resurgence

From ashes cold, a heartbeat stirs,
In whispers soft, the memory blurs.
Crimson threads in twilight's weave,
Awakening hope for those who believe.

With gentle breaths, the daylight grows,
Night's bitter grip begins to close.
Fragile blooms in sacred ground,
Resilience found in the lost and bound.

Through tangled fears, light finds a way,
In fleeting moments that night gives sway.
In every tear, a story sown,
The fragile hearts have brightly grown.

Emerging strong, from shadows cast,
The future calls, tying the past.
In every whisper, the promise yearns,
From fragile lives, the fire returns.

## Embrace of the Radiant Flame

In the anchor light of evening's glow,
The radiant flame dances slow.
Each flicker whispers, each shadow sings,
A warm embrace of the warmth it brings.

Lost in brilliance, souls converge,
Together forged in the fire's surge.
In laughter bright, in sorrow deep,
The radiant flame, a bond to keep.

Through thickest night, a beacon bright,
Guiding hearts with its gentle light.
In unity's warmth, we face the storm,
In embrace of flame, we find our form.

With every heartbeat, love's immortal spark,
Ignites the dark with a lasting mark.
In the embers held within our hands,
The radiant flame, forever stands.

## Threads of Skyward Resilience

In twilight's glance, the stars align,
Whispers of dreams in shadows entwine.
Each heartbeat sings, each breath we take,
Threads of hope weave, never to break.

With courage sewn in twilight's seam,
We climb the heights, we chase the gleam.
Mountains bow to the strength inside,
In every soul, a comet's ride.

The winds may gale, the storms may roar,
But deep within, we're meant for more.
With every fall, we rise anew,
Resilience shines in skies so blue.

## Flames That Whisper

In dusky fields where shadows creep,
The flames of hope begin to leap.
They dance like secrets in the night,
Whispers of warmth, a guiding light.

With every ember, stories blend,
A promise forged, a heart to mend.
We gather close to share our dreams,
In the dark, our courage gleams.

Through trials faced and fears we brace,
The fire within ignites our grace.
No wind can snuff what fate will bear,
For in our hearts, the flame is rare.

## Tapestry of Rising Beams

In morning's blush, new colors call,
Threads of gold across the hall.
A tapestry, woven with care,
Hope and love in every snare.

With hands of toil and hearts aflame,
We stitch our dreams, we claim our name.
From shadows cast, our laughter springs,
In every thread, the joy it brings.

When daylight fades, and night descends,
The beams of light become our friends.
Together we weave, together we rise,
In the tapestry, a world of skies.

## Sparked by Destiny's Loom

In the loom of fate where dreams ignite,
Threads of time weave day and night.
Stars align to craft our way,
As destinies in silence sway.

Beneath the moon's soft, guiding glance,
We find our voice, we take our chance.
With every knot, a story spun,
In colors bright, our journey's begun.

The loom may twist, the weave may fray,
Yet in our hearts, the spark will stay.
With every breath, the future looms,
In the fabric rich, our spirit blooms.

## **Flare of the Reborn Heart**

In shadows deep where echoes sigh,
A heart reborn begins to fly.
With every flame, a whisper heard,
A tale of hope, in dreams deferred.

From ashes cool, new embers spark,
As courage wakes within the dark.
Each heartbeat marks a path anew,
The courage found to push on through.

With every tear, a lesson learned,
In whispered winds, a love returned.
The night must fade, and morning rise,
To light the path beyond the skies.

So let the fire dance and leap,
For in its warmth, the soul does keep.
A story forged in flames so bright,
The reborn heart ignites the night.

Through trials faced and battles fought,
In every failure, courage caught.
The flare of life, both fierce and true,
In every breath, a spark anew.

## The Phoenix of Starlit Weavings

In twilight's arms, the phoenix sleeps,
Amongst the stars, its promise keeps.
With swirling night, the tales unwind,
Of woven dreams and fates entwined.

Through cosmic threads, the heavens churn,
A heart aflame, for flight it yearns.
In tapestry of dreams unspun,
The phoenix rises with the sun.

Each feather bright, a story told,
In colors bold, both warm and cold.
From dust and flame, a life reborn,
A dance of light, a new day dawn.

The starlit skies, a canvas vast,
With every heartbeat, shadows cast.
Yet through the night, the fire glows,
From ashes fierce, the spirit grows.

So herald forth, the dawn, the light,
In every soul, a spark ignites.
The phoenix soars on wings of grace,
In starlit weavings, find your place.

## Heartstrings of Ashen Beauty

In silent woods where shadows dwell,
A melody begins to swell.
With every breeze, a haunting tune,
The heartstrings pull beneath the moon.

From ashes old, the echoes rise,
In whispered words, the spirit flies.
Each note a thread, in twilight spun,
The ashen beauty, lost but won.

With every sigh, a tale unfolds,
Of love once bright, now bittersweet gold.
Yet in the dusk, new songs arise,
With every tear, a phoenix flies.

The heartstrings strum, a gentle call,
To those who rise, and those who fall.
Through every scar, a beauty gleams,
In woven tales of whispered dreams.

So take the path where shadows lie,
And let your spirit learn to fly.
For in the ash, the truth is found,
In heartstrings' grip, love's sweetest sound.

## The Fire's Gentle Tapestry

Weaving warmth with threads of gold,
A tapestry of tales retold.
With flickers bright and shadows deep,
The fire sighs, and dreams it keeps.

In tranquil nights, the embers glow,
A gentle dance, a rhythmic flow.
Each spark a wish, a hope released,
In every flame, the heart finds peace.

The tapestry unfolds with grace,
In every fold, a secret place.
Through weary hours and silent fears,
The fire whispers through the years.

So gather close, let stories thread,
In flames of warmth, no words unsaid.
The fire's gentle glow composes,
A melody of love's soft poses.

With every flicker, a truth we find,
In shadows long, our hearts aligned.
For in the warmth of friendship's glee,
The fire's tapestry sets us free.

## Embers Entwined in Cosmic Woven Dreams

In twilight's hush, the embers glow,
A dance of sparks, both fast and slow.
They weave through tales of distant night,
In cosmic cloak, they spread their light.

A tapestry of fate unfolds,
In whispered secrets, silence holds.
With every flicker, dreams take flight,
As starlit visions bless the night.

The universe sings with ancient sound,
In every heartbeat, magic's found.
The fire's heat, both fierce and kind,
Ignites the souls, their hopes entwined.

Together bound, like moon and tide,
In fiery waltz, we will abide.
With every ember, we shall soar,
Through woven dreams forevermore.

## The Resurgence of Spiraling Starlight

In velvet skies where starlight twirls,
A sparkling dance, as fate unfurls.
From depths of night, new visions rise,
In swirling tides of endless skies.

Galaxies spin with fiery grace,
A cosmic waltz, a boundless place.
Each star reborn, a light anew,
In vast expanse, we find our crew.

The universe, a canvas wide,
With radiant hues, our dreams collide.
In spirals bright, we seek our spark,
Illuminated paths through dark.

Together we chart the endless ways,
In starlit journeys, endless plays.
Embrace the dance, let spirits glide,
In the resurgence where love abides.

## Flames Ushering New Heights

In shadows deep, a flicker glows,
A dance of fire, where courage grows.
Each spark ignites a dream held tight,
Together we'll soar, into the night.

With blazing hearts, we chase the stars,
Our spirits strong, we'll break the bars.
Through trials hard, and storms we'll ride,
With flames of hope, we'll turn the tide.

Unfurl your wings, embrace the blaze,
In whispered winds, we'll find our ways.
March forth, dear souls, with heads held high,
For from the flames, we learn to fly.

In every ember, there's a tale,
Of love and loss, of how we fail.
Yet in the ashes, new life springs,
From charred remains, the phoenix sings.

So let the flames guide our ascent,
To heights unseen, in hearts we'll vent.
With every blaze, we grow more wise,
In fire's glow, our spirits rise.

### Echoes of the Ember Song

In twilight hush, the embers hum,
A melody born from fire's thumb.
With every crackle, the stories weave,
Of dreams ignited, of those who believe.

Whispers of warmth and light persist,
In shadows deep, they still exist.
A symphony of flames, bright and strong,
Resonates deep within the throng.

Face forward now, let spirits sway,
To the echoing song that leads the way.
In smoky trails, our hopes take flight,
Guided by stars that kiss the night.

Hold fast the notes that flicker bright,
For in their heart, lies endless light.
With every rise, our souls reborn,
In the ember's glow, we shall adorn.

So let the song be heard afar,
A beacon bright, a guiding star.
In unity, our hearts engage,
To the echo of the ember's page.

## Resilient Wings in Dawn's Light

As morning breaks, the shadows flee,
With gentle rays, the world we see.
Beneath the sky, with colors bold,
Our stories rise, in light retold.

The wings we bear, a strength so pure,
Imbued with hope, they shall endure.
Through valleys deep and mountains high,
We spread our wings, we learn to fly.

Each dawn a chance to start anew,
With whispered dreams, we'll push on through.
For every fall, we learn to rise,
With vibrant hearts, unbound, we strive.

In nature's breath, we find our way,
Guided by light, through night and day.
Resilience blooms in every heart,
With every step, we play our part.

So let the dawn ignite our flame,
Unshackle doubt, embrace our name.
With every flight, together we stand,
In dawn's embrace, we'll build our land.

## Strands of Celestial Rebirth

In cosmic realms, a tapestry glows,
With threads of light, our journey flows.
Each strand a story, woven with care,
Of love and loss laid ever bare.

The stardust whispers of ages gone,
A cycle of life, in dusk and dawn.
From ashes rise, a phoenix fair,
In every heart, the embers share.

With every pulse of the universe,
We find our place, despite the curse.
In celestial dance, we seek the truth,
Of dreams reborn in eternal youth.

The moon will guide, the sun will cheer,
Through every trial, we'll persevere.
For in this web, our souls unite,
In harmony's glow, we claim our right.

So let the strands of fate entwine,
In cosmic light, our paths align.
With wings of hope, forever soar,
To realms of love, forever more.

## Echoes of Eternal Flight

In the twilight's tender glow,
Souls take wing, where shadows flow,
Among the stars, their whispers blend,
In flights that never seem to end.

Every heartbeat marks a trace,
Of dreams that time cannot erase,
Through realms where hearts and hopes ignite,
In echoes of eternal flight.

Beneath the moon's watchful eye,
Wings unfurl as spirits sigh,
Searching skies for tales untold,
In a tapestry of gold.

The nightingale sings sweet and clear,
To the winds that draw it near,
A symphony of love and loss,
In every rise, a measured toss.

So soar, dear travelers, and find,
The silver lining, intertwined,
With every echo, every spark,
In the vast expanse of dark.

## The Dance of Molten Feathers

In the forge of dreams, we dance,
Spirits twirling in a trance,
Feathers gleam with ember's light,
Crafting magic through the night.

Upon the anvil of the heart,
Each pulse, a spark, a work of art,
Molten colors, bright and bold,
Stories of the brave and old.

The flames whisper secrets low,
In the rhythm, fire's glow,
With every pivot, souls entwine,
In the warmth of dreams divine.

Bright horizons calling near,
Through the heat, they persevere,
In the dance, each feather falls,
A testament that love enthralls.

So gather 'round, let spirits soar,
In the heat, we seek for more,
For the dance of molten dreams,
Shapes the world in radiant beams.

## Rising From Forgotten Ashes

From the embers of the past,
New beginnings rise at last,
In the silence left behind,
Whispers of the heart, entwined.

Ashen memories, softly fade,
Yet in their wake, foundations laid,
Hope ignites like morning dew,
In the shadows, life anew.

Through the wreckage, sparks ignite,
Hearts awaken to the light,
Each breath a promise, fiercely bold,
A tale of courage to be told.

With strength like wings of ancient lore,
We rise above, forevermore,
From forgotten ashes, we create,
A destiny, a fateful state.

So lift your gaze, embrace the skies,
For in your heart, the phoenix lies,
In every rise, a story spun,
Of dreams reborn and battles won.

## Whispers of the Flame's Heart

In the depths where secrets dwell,
The flame's heart casts its spell,
Softly whispering through the night,
A glow that dances, pure delight.

Echoes of a fire's embrace,
Rising tides of warmth and grace,
Each flicker tells a tale of old,
Of heroes brave and spirits bold.

Through the shadows, secrets weave,
In the comfort they believe,
A gentle warmth in winter's chill,
Awakening the deepest will.

So listen close; let silence guide,
To the heart where dreams reside,
In whispers held by flame's soft breath,
The dance of life, defying death.

Each ember holds a wish anew,
In the heart where love breaks through,
In the quiet, find your art,
And cherish whispers of the heart.

## Threads of Twilight in the Realm of Fire

In shadows deep, the whispers wane,
Threads of twilight weave the pain.
With each spark, a story glows,
In the realm where silence grows.

Fire dances, a fierce ballet,
Ember's grace, at dusk they play.
Flickering visions, secrets bare,
Through the twilight's tender care.

Try as we might, to hold the night,
Yet dawn creeps soft, a soothing light.
In flames we forge, in shadows we trust,
The twilight weeps, return to dust.

## Embers in the Weave

In strands of fate, embers gleam,
A tapestry of sullen dreams.
Each thread connects, a tale unknown,
In whispered breaths, our spirits moan.

Through the darkness, shadows creep,
In the silence, secrets keep.
A flicker here, a glow there bright,
In the loom, we weave our plight.

Burning softly, yet fierce as fire,
We chase desires, we feel the pyre.
In every spark, a chance reborn,
In twilight's arms, we stand forlorn.

## Wings of a Rebirth

A phoenix flies, its wings expand,
In azure skies where dreams command.
From ash and smoke, life gathers steam,
Wings of rebirth, realizing a dream.

Through crimson clouds, it soars anew,
In every heartbeat, the ancient view.
A tender grace, each plume ablaze,
In the dawn's light, our spirits gaze.

Higher still, to the heavens call,
In flight we rise, refusing the fall.
With every flap, the past released,
In winged embrace, our souls are pleased.

## Ascent from Ashen Dreams

From smoldering ruins, hope takes flight,
In ashen dreams, we seek the light.
Through whispered prayers, our hearts ignite,
An ascent born from the bitter night.

With every step, the shadows fade,
In twilight's grip, our futures laid.
Together we rise, spirits entwined,
With courage chiseled, fate aligned.

The ashes swirl, a dance of grace,
In the weave of time, we find our place.
From searing losses, we gently glean,
In the echo of hopes, we reign supreme.

### Flames that chart the Celestial Mirage

In the hush of night, they blaze,
Hot tongues that whisper tales of stars.
They dance against the darkened maze,
Reflecting dreams from worlds afar.

A canvas filled with fiery hues,
Each flicker speaks of age-old lore.
Their vibrant strokes, a cosmic muse,
Awakening what came before.

From distant realms their warmth descends,
They conjure visions, wild and free.
As time unwinds, the wonder bends,
A tapestry of mystery.

With every crackle, secrets churn,
In swirling motions, light unfurls.
The universe begins to learn,
Through flames, the heart of night twirls.

So let the embers guide your flight,
Through constellations, paths bespoke.
In flames that chart the endless night,
Find solace in the magic's cloak.

## Mysteries Born from the Ashen Gaze

Beneath the cloak of shadowed flight,
The ashes whisper tales untold.
A gaze that pierces through the night,
Holds treasures worth their weight in gold.

In every spark, a memory glows,
Flickering with the weight of time.
The silence brews, and still it flows,
Across the canvas, dark yet prime.

Lost echoes linger in the air,
With stories waiting to ignite.
The ashes hum, a quiet prayer,
Unveiling what it hides from sight.

Through ashen haze, a vision formed,
Of heroes lost and legends grand.
In subtle warmth, new dreams are warmed,
A touch of fate, a guiding hand.

As dusk consumes the fading light,
Embrace the mystery unfurled.
For in the ashes dwells the fight,
Unraveling the veils of worlds.

## Phoenix Hearth: A Chronicle of Renewal

From embers low, a flame will rise,
A phoenix drawn from ashes' bed.
With fiery wings that touch the skies,
It soars above where few have tread.

In every cycle, life reborn,
A tale of loss, a tale of gain.
From fiery storm to brightening dawn,
In mystery, the heart won't wane.

The hearth of hope, where dreams converge,
With every dawn, a chance to grow.
As night recedes, the spirits surge,
Rekindling what we thought we'd know.

Through trials faced and battles fought,
The phoenix sings of what's to come.
In every lesson, wisdom taught,
The heart beats strong, no longer numb.

So let the embers spark your flame,
And rise again with steadfast grace.
In every life, a new name,
A journey bold through time and space.

## Sculpting Light from the Ember's Remains

In the quietude of fading fire,
From coldest ashes, warmth will swell.
Though night may cloak, deep hidden desire,
Whispers of hope begin to dwell.

With careful hands, we mold the light,
From remnants of what once could be.
An artist's touch ignites the night,
Creating worlds for eyes to see.

Each ember gleams with spirit's might,
A glimmering testament to life.
In shadows cast, we find our sight,
Emerging through the depths of strife.

The darkness holds a fragile glow,
A beacon for the weary soul.
With every breath, the flames do grow,
Enkindling dreams to make us whole.

So gather 'round the glowing hearth,
And let the light reshape the way.
In every heart, a treasure's worth,
Sculpting joy from what once was gray.

## Embered Wings and the Caravan of Stars

In the night sky's gentle embrace,
Embers dance with a fleeting grace.
Caravans travel on dreams so bright,
Guided by whispers of silver light.

Through the cosmos a soft tune plays,
A melody tracing the starlit ways.
Wings of fire flutter, drawing near,
Carrying wishes, all hopes sincere.

Over mountains of swirling mist,
Secrets woven with each sun-kissed tryst.
An adventure awaits in the dreams unfurled,
Where magic and wonder meet the world.

Beneath the glow of a shimmering sun,
Stories gather, their threads spun.
Each star a tale, each twinkle a spark,
Lighting the paths as we venture dark.

So take flight on embered wings,
Join the caravan, hear what it brings.
For in the night, the heart does soar,
To realms unknown, forevermore.

## Threads of Destiny Woven in Crimson

In shadows deep, the loom does spin,
Crimson threads where tales begin.
Fates entwined in a tapestry vast,
Echoes of futures and whispers of past.

Each stitch a story, a life bestowed,
In the fabric of time, destiny flowed.
With hands of fate, we weave and mend,
In the quiet hours, where dreams ascend.

Through the dark, a flash of light,
Guiding souls in the endless night.
With every heartbeat, the threads align,
Crafting a journey, a life divine.

The loom still hums with tales untold,
Of love, of loss, of dreams so bold.
In crimson glow, our paths are spun,
Embracing the battles that must be won.

So take a thread, let it weave anew,
In the tapestry bright, where stars break through.
For destinies shift with each passing hour,
In the hands of time, we hold the power.

## The Ascendant Mirage of Rejuvenation

In the dawn's breath, a mirage blooms,
Whispers of life in forgotten rooms.
Each ray a promise, a second chance,
Where souls rekindle and shadows dance.

A river flows with restless dreams,
Mirrored reflections and vibrant gleams.
In the garden of hopes, new shoots arise,
Beneath the watchful, ancient skies.

From ashes born, a spirit sings,
Claiming the joy that each dawn brings.
In the tapestry of life, we find our place,
Rejuvenated souls in an endless race.

Listen closely to the vibrant hum,
The pulse of the earth, the beating drum.
With each step forward, a new road unfurls,
Filling our hearts with the magic of worlds.

So embrace the light that flickers anew,
In the spirit of change, we break through.
For in each mirage, a truth will rise,
A testament written in the skies.

## Echoes of the Eternal Inferno

In the depths of night, the fire breathes,
An eternal dance, all sorrow sheaves.
Echoes roar in the hollow heart,
Flames that flicker, never to part.

Cinders whisper tales of yore,
Of battles fought and endless lore.
Each spark ignites a story anew,
In the forge of fate, we kindle true.

Through the smoke, a vision lies,
Dreams entwined with the ash that flies.
In the inferno's core, we find our will,
Turning the warmth into a chill.

Yet from the blaze, life's colors pour,
Healing wounds we thought were sore.
In every ember, a promise stays,
A legacy born from fiery rays.

So heed the echoes that softly call,
In the depths of darkness, we rise or fall.
For in the inferno, we find our light,
Eternal flames that banish the night.

**From Scorched Echoes, New Beginnings Rise**

From ashes lost, a whisper born,
A tale of hope in twilight's scorn.
The past may blaze with fiery darts,
Yet embered dreams can mend our hearts.

In silent sighs, the shadows breathe,
A fragrant bloom through burnt-out sheathe.
With every end, a chance to soar,
To forge anew on fate's wide shore.

The echoes of what once was here,
Compose a song of love, not fear.
Those charred remains, a soil so rich,
From it arises a heart's true pitch.

When darkness pulls with heavy hands,
We find our strength in shifting sands.
The brightest stars from night are spun,
In every loss, a victory won.

So gather 'round, brave souls and kin,
For every end brings light within.
From scorched echoes, life shall rise,
With wings of gold against the skies.

## Tapestry of a Fabled Rebirth

Threads of fate in woven dance,
A tapestry of chance and glance.
Each color bright, a story spun,
Of olden days and battles won.

With every stitch, our legends bloom,
In shadows lurk both joy and doom.
Yet through the cracks, a shimmer shines,
A promise kept in ancient lines.

The weaver hums a lilting song,
Of heroes bold who righted wrong.
Their echoes linger, sweet yet stark,
As morning light ignites the dark.

In woven tales, we find our way,
Through dusky nights and brightening day.
With every thread, a hope refined,
A fabled rebirth of humankind.

Together bound, we rise and roam,
In every heart, a place called home.
The tapestry speaks of love and strife,
In every weave, the pulse of life.

**Flights of Fire Beneath the Velvet Sky**

Beneath the stars, the dragons soar,
With fiery breath, they seek for more.
A dance of flames, the night ignites,
In swirling mists, a love takes flight.

Across the heavens, they twist and turn,
In ashen clouds, the embers burn.
Each beat of wings, a thunderous sound,
In velvet night, their dreams unbound.

The moonlight casts a silver sheen,
Upon the realms where they have been.
In whispered winds, their stories shared,
Of boundless skies, and hearts laid bare.

As dawn approaches, shadows flee,
Yet through the light their spirits see.
For every flight beneath this dome,
Resides the fire that leads us home.

So watch the skies, believe the lore,
For in their flight, we find our core.
In smoky trails, passion does lie,
In every breath, a daring high.

## **Shimmering Scales of a Fiery Awakening**

In depths of dusk, a glimmer shines,
With scales that echo time's designs.
Through molten seas, the legends twine,
In fiery hues, their fates align.

With shimmering light, they greet the dawn,
Emerging proud upon the lawn.
From slumber deep, they rise anew,
With hearts ablaze, their spirits true.

Each scale, a story, bold and bright,
Of battles fought and endless flight.
With every flick, the darkness fades,
In warmth of sun, their dreams cascade.

The world awaits, with bated breath,
For fire's song to dance with death.
In twilight's glow, a truth awakens,
With every heartbeat, love unshaken.

So heed the call, O listeners dear,
To shimmering scales that draw us near.
For in their rise, we too embrace,
The fiery spirit in our grace.

## Embers of the Ascendant Spirit

In the heart where shadows blend,
A whisper calls, a light to send.
From ashes deep, the dreams ignite,
The spirit soars beyond the night.

With every spark, a tale begins,
Of battles fought and bitter sins.
Yet hope emerges, fierce and bright,
Guiding souls to realms of light.

The stars align, the heavens hum,
As courage blooms where fear was sown.
Together we shall rise again,
Embers dance, becomes the flame.

Through winding paths, our fates entwined,
In silent strength, we seek and find.
The echoes of our past resound,
In every heart, a truth is found.

So lift your gaze, let spirits soar,
Beyond the veil, to evermore.
In unity, we carve the stars,
The embers spark, our journey's ours.

## The Phoenix's Silent Song

In the dimmest dawn, a hush prevails,
The phoenix wakes, through whispers sails.
With wings of flame, she stirs the day,
A silent song that sweeps away.

From ashes' hold, a voice so clear,
Soft as a prayer, strong as a steer.
She sings of hope, of endless flight,
A melody that warms the night.

In every heart, a spark resides,
In darkest times, the spirit guides.
With every note, a promise grown,
In unity, we find our throne.

Through trials faced, through tears we shed,
The phoenix flies, where dreams are bred.
Together we'll rise, as one, we dare,
In silent song, we find our prayer.

So heed her call, let courage swell,
In every heart, a tale to tell.
For in the ashes, we will sing,
The phoenix's song, a flame takes wing.

## Threads Woven in Firelight

In twilight's glow, where shadows play,
We weave our tales, both night and day.
With threads of gold and silver bright,
In firelight's warmth, we forge our plight.

Through tempests fierce and storms that roar,
Our stories bind, forevermore.
With every stitch, our hopes align,
In fabric rich, our dreams entwine.

From whispered words to laughter shared,
Each moment cherished, deeply dared.
In woven threads, our hearts embrace,
A tapestry of time and space.

Together, strong, we stand as one,
With every thread, a journey spun.
In firelight's glow, the past unveils,
A radiant spark that never pales.

So gather 'round, let tales ignite,
In woven dreams, we face the night.
With every seam, our spirits rise,
In firelight's embrace, we touch the skies.

## **Flight Beyond the Ember's Edge**

Where embers glow, and shadows fade,
We find the path, our fears allayed.
With every breath, a courage known,
Together we shall carve our throne.

Beneath the moon, where whispers dwell,
We hear the tales that stars could tell.
In twilight's grasp, our spirits soar,
Beyond the edge, to lands of more.

With fiery hearts, we chase the dawn,
In every leap, a new hope drawn.
Through trials faced, our strength revealed,
In unity, our fates are sealed.

So take my hand, let's rise above,
In every heartbeat, truth and love.
Together we'll break the chains that bind,
And find our way through worlds unkind.

For in the flight, our souls unite,
Through ember's edge, we grasp the light.
With spirits bold, and eyes ablaze,
We chase the stars, through endless maze.

## **Radiant Threads of Fate**

In twilight's glow, the threads unwind,
A tapestry of lives entwined,
With colors bright, in shadows cast,
We weave our dreams, both slow and fast.

Through whispered winds, the secrets flow,
Each turn of fate, a gentle blow,
With sturdy hands, we shape our path,
In every choice, the aftermath.

The guiding stars, they shine above,
Unraveling tales of hope and love,
As laughter dances on the breeze,
We find our strength amidst the trees.

When darkness falls, the threads grow tight,
Yet in the gloom, we seek the light,
Together bound by fate's embrace,
We carve our names in time and space.

So fear not futures yet unknown,
In every thread, a seed is sown,
With radiant hope, let hearts not wait,
For every moment shall create.

## The Loom Beneath the Fire

A flicker bright, the hearth does glow,
Beneath its warmth, the dreams will grow,
In secret corners, shadows play,
While whispers weave the night away.

The loom of life, it twists and bends,
With every thread, the story mends,
A tapestry of night and day,
Where hopes and fears in silence sway.

Through patterned fabric, visions gleam,
In quiet hours, we chase a dream,
The flames will dance, the ties will bind,
As every stitch unites the mind.

In this cocoon, where fates align,
We find the solace that's divine,
For every spark ignites a chance,
In loom's embrace, our spirits dance.

So gather close, let tales unfold,
With words spun from the heart of gold,
As ember light and shadows blend,
We forge our fate, our stories mend.

## **Ember Dreams and Starlit Hopes**

In the hush of night, dreams take flight,
Embers glow, a soft delight,
While starlit wishes pierce the dark,
In quiet hearts, ignites a spark.

Whispers drift on gentle air,
Carrying secrets, light as hair,
With every breath, the cosmos sings,
Of hopes entwined on silver strings.

The fire's dance, a fleeting glow,
Reflects the dreams we yearn to know,
As shadows stretch and time unfolds,
The mysteries of futures told.

Through silvered nights and golden morns,
Our ember dreams, like phoenixes, are born,
In starlit skies, our wishes bloom,
Banishing the weight of gloom.

So take a chance, let moments flow,
Embrace the light, let spirits grow,
For in the night where dreams ignite,
We find our path, our hearts in flight.

## Interlacing Wings and Wishes

With wings of hope, we soar on high,
In skies of blue, where dreams don't die,
Each whispered wish, a feathered grace,
Lifts us gently from our place.

In swirling winds, our spirits blend,
As time unravels, journeys send,
Through endless skies, our hearts will chase,
The mysteries held in space.

The lightest touch of morning dawn,
Brings dreams alive, though night has gone,
With every beat, our wishes rise,
In harmony beneath the skies.

Yet even in the storms we face,
We'll find our way, embrace the pace,
For wings interlaced will guide us through,
In every trial, a bond so true.

So lend your heart to the winds of fate,
As wishes soar, we navigate,
Together bound, in flight we trust,
Interlacing wings, fulfill we must.

## Flames in the Fabric of Night

In the hush of night, shadows weave,
Whispers of secrets, that time won't leave.
A flicker of fire, a spark of hope,
In darkness we find ways to cope.

Threads of embers dance in the air,
A tapestry formed with tender care.
Under the moon's soft, watchful gaze,
We find our way through the misty haze.

Crimson trails across the deep blue,
Illuminating dreams that feel so true.
The flames unite, they twist and twine,
Crafting a song, a tale divine.

Souls intertwine like threads of gold,
In this night of stories yet untold.
In warmth's embrace, we boldly tread,
Following paths where angels thread.

As dawn breaks forth, flames softly die,
But the fabric remains, rising high.
In the light of day, hearts will ignite,
Forever dancing in the fabric of night.

## The Weaver's Fiery Symphony

In a realm where magic deftly sings,
A weaver crafts with vibrant strings.
Each thread a tale, each color a dream,
Woven in harmony, they shimmer and gleam.

From the loom arise flames fierce and bright,
Dancing to rhythms that thrill the night.
The air is alive with sparks that fly,
A symphony played 'neath the starlit sky.

Gold and crimson spiral and twine,
Interlacing fate with a design.
With every note, the music swells,
Echoing softly like distant bells.

Through fire and shadow, the weaver moves,
Crafting the world where mystery grooves.
In twilight's embrace, the magic thrives,
Awakening dreams, where imagination dives.

The final thread, a flourish of grace,
A tapestry woven time cannot erase.
In the hearts of those who dare to believe,
The weaver's fiery symphony will never leave.

## **Resurgence Under Starlit Skies**

When dusk descends and stars align,
The night awakens, a chance to shine.
From ashes borne, a spirit climbs,
In whispers carried by ancient rhymes.

Under the canopy of twinkling lights,
Fires reignite, warming the nights.
In the vast expanse where fears take flight,
Hope unfurls like wings, pure and bright.

A phoenix rises, shedding the past,
Transforming pain, a shadow cast.
With every heartbeat, the world revives,
In the embrace of night, the soul thrives.

Through trials faced in silence and tears,
Strength emerges, dissolving fears.
Under starlit skies, we forge anew,
Resilience blooms in vibrant hues.

As dawn approaches, gilding the sky,
A promise lingers, we shall not die.
In every heartbeat, the night's reprise,
A resurgence of life under starlit skies.

## Flames of Transformation

In the heart of dusk, shadows convene,
A flicker ignites where the unseen.
Transformation whispers with crackling cheer,
Flames of passion that banish fear.

From the embers, a glow will rise,
Illuminating dreams like starlit skies.
Colors blend in a wild embrace,
Each flicker a step in a daring chase.

Time shifts and bends in the fire's dance,
A chance for growth, a final glance.
Through the heat, we shed the old,
Emerging anew, as stories unfold.

A tapestry woven in fiery hues,
Life's vibrant journey infused with clues.
In the forge of night, we'll break the mold,
With flames of transformation burning bold.

As dawn unveils its tender light,
The whispers of night take flight.
With every flame that flickers and sways,
We find our path in the new day's gaze.

## **Phoenix Flight Beyond the Night**

In shadows deep, a spark ignites,
A feathery form in the moon's soft light.
With wings of gold, it soars so high,
A legend reborn, beneath the sky.

Through whispers of flames, the fire sings,
Resilience blooms in the heart of things.
From ashes gray, its spirit soars,
A tale of courage forever endures.

With each dawn's glow, a promise made,
The night retreats, as dreams invade.
Hold tight your hopes, let them unite,
For in the dark, begins the flight.

Around the stars, it waltzes free,
A symbol of hope for you and me.
In the heart of the night, see it rise,
A phoenix born under celestial skies.

So when you feel the weight of despair,
Look to the heavens, find warmth in air.
For every end is a brand new start,
Let the phoenix ignite your heart.

## Spark of the Infinite Sky

Glimmers of light pierce the dark,
A whisper of magic leaves its mark.
In the tapestry of endless dreams,
Stars hold the secrets, or so it seems.

Each twinkle tells of a story spun,
Of journeys taken and battles won.
The vast expanse, both wild and free,
Holds the promise of what's yet to be.

As night descends, the canvas waits,
A spark ignites, as destiny creates.
Beyond the horizon, where shadows fade,
Hope lights the path, unafraid.

With wonder, gaze at the starry sea,
Each sparkling light calls out to thee.
From depths of silence, a wish takes flight,
Carried on wings of the infinite night.

So trust your heart, let dreams unfold,
For within the dark, lies treasure untold.
Embrace the magic that lives inside,
Awaken the spark, let hope be your guide.

## Threads of Fire and Spirit

Weaving through shadows, a flame takes lead,
Threads of fire in embers plead.
With every flicker, a story breathe,
In the heart of darkness, the spirit weaves.

Tangled in battles, yet softly kissed,
The warmth of hope you cannot resist.
With courage sewn into every seam,
Find solace in the embrace of dreams.

From ashes of yesterday's pain,
Rise anew, like a gentle rain.
Each strand pulsing with life and light,
Binding the past with future bright.

Let the fire guide, let the spirit fly,
Embrace the chaos of the night sky.
For in the dance of flame and air,
You'll find your strength, beyond compare.

Together we forge, a tapestry grand,
With threads of spirit, we hand in hand.
Through trials and triumphs, we'll find the way,
As the night melts into day.

## **Shimmering Tapestry of Rebirth**

In the cradle of twilight, colors blend,
A tale of rebirth that never ends.
Threads of the past, woven so fine,
Create a fabric where futures entwine.

With every heartbeat, a rhythm plays,
Painting the canvas of life's endless maze.
Through the storms that twist and bend,
Hope rises anew, as night's shadows end.

Glimmers of light spring forth from dark,
Writing the stories that ignite a spark.
Each twinkle whispers the dreams we hold,
A shimmering promise in shades of gold.

As dawn awakens, colors ignite,
A tapestry shining, pure and bright.
With threads of joy and strands of grace,
We weave together in time and space.

Embrace the journey of life's sweet art,
For every ending brings a new start.
Together, we'll dance in the vibrant light,
In a shimmering tapestry of rebirth's flight.

## The Infinity Loop of Burning Ascension

In the heart of a flame, where shadows wane,
Echoes of destiny whisper the strain.
Spirals of time, entwined in their dance,
Burning with purpose, igniting romance.

Each flicker a story, from ashes it swells,
Carried by whispers of magical spells.
Through cycles of trials, our spirits take flight,
Ascending like phoenixes, radiant and bright.

A twist of the fate, on the edge of despair,
Embers of hope linger, flickering rare.
The loop ever turning, a timeless embrace,
We rise from the ruins, our true selves to face.

Eternal the journey, through chaos and flame,
In the circle of burning, we're all still the same.
For love is the fire that fuels us anew,
In this infinity loop, forever we grew.

## Dreams Forged in the Crucible of Fire

Within the forge of the night, dreams ignite,
Molten desires swirl, ever taking flight.
In the crucible's heart, we face all our fears,
Shaping our futures while shedding our tears.

Wrought in the fire, the anvil of fate,
Strengthened by trials, we learn to create.
Each vision a jewel, each heartbeat a chime,
Resilient as flame, transcending through time.

With starlit ambitions, we rise from the heat,
To dance with the sparks and the rhythm's beat.
Dreams forged in the dark, like lanterns they glow,
Illuminating paths where only few go.

In the chambers of night, where shadows collide,
We craft our tomorrows with passion and pride.
For within every ember, a new world awakes,
In our crucible moments, our spirit partakes.

## The Celestial Loom of Reincarnation

In the tapestry woven with threads of the stars,
Life's cycles unfold, with their luminous scars.
Each stitch a reminder, of journeys we've known,
Through worlds we have traveled, all colors have grown.

Patterns emerging, as time weaves along,
In the loom of existence, we sing our song.
From whispers of stardust, to echoes of light,
We dance through the ages, in endless delight.

Past lives entwined in the fabric of fate,
Rebirths like morning, as shadows abate.
In each precious moment, we gather the threads,
Stitching our stories where the universe spreads.

As we drift on the winds of celestial grace,
In the loom's gentle tug, we find our place.
For every new chapter, a tale to embrace,
In the eternal weave, we're a part of the space.

# Celestial Kites Dancing on Fiery Winds

Up high in the heavens, where stars take their flight,
Celestial kites soar, a magnificent sight.
They twirl on the breezes of fate's playful hand,
Braving the tempest, they boldly will stand.

Colors of sunrise, in the skies they entwine,
Dancing with shadows where day meets divine.
Each tug of the string is a heartbeat set free,
A tapestry soaring, like dreams of the sea.

With wild gusts of passion, through clouds they flit,
Chasing the essence of freedom they sit.
In the warmth of the sun, they lift, leap, and glide,
Whispering secrets where the cosmos abide.

On fiery winds, they shimmer and spin,
A testament glowing to the strength within.
For even in storms, they refuse to fall,
Harnessing magic, in unity, all.

Beneath the vast canvas, where wonders align,
Celestial kites dance, in rhythm, divine.
In every swirl, we find courage anew,
Writing our tales in the skies' endless blue.

## **A Tangle of Forgotten Echoes**

In the whispering woods, shadows play,
Memories dance in the misty gray.
Promises lost where the wildflowers bloom,
Time swirls the ages into a delicate loom.

Faint laughter lingers, a ghostly chime,
Stories entwined, echo through time.
The secrets of old buried deep in the ground,
Awakening softly, in silence profound.

Beneath ancient trees, the whispers reside,
Of dreams long forsaken, now lost with pride.
The moon's gentle light weaves through the night,
Revealing the tales that dwell just out of sight.

In the heart of the forest, shadows convene,
Where time slips away, and the world feels serene.
A tangle of echoes, both haunting and sweet,
In every soft rustle, old spirits repeat.

So heed the soft call, let the echoes flow,
In the weave of the woods where forgotten things grow.
For every small whisper, a tale is spun,
And the dance of the past is never quite done.

## Ashen Hues of Vibrant Dawn

In the cradle of dusk, the night softly sighs,
Painting the skies with ashen goodbyes.
Yet from the horizon, a promise unfolds,
A vibrant dawn waiting, beckoning bold.

Rays break the silence, a warm golden hue,
Brushing the world with a tender renew.
The shadows retreat as the day starts to gleam,
Whispers of hope in the soft morning beam.

Birds stretch their wings as the sun starts to climb,
Chasing the echoes of yesterday's time.
With each gentle stroke, the colors ignite,
Transforming the canvas, the darkness takes flight.

Among the soft petals, the dew gleams like gold,
Stories of life in the blossoms unfold.
Ashen hues fade, as the world comes alive,
In the heart of the dawn, every spirit will thrive.

So stand at the edge of this splendid array,
Let the vibrant dawn chase the ashes away.
For hope springs eternal, in each new sunrise,
A tapestry woven with dreams in the skies.

## The Flight of Phoenix's Dream

In the ember glow where the flames start to dance,
A phoenix rises, reborn from a chance.
With feathers of gold that shimmer and shine,
Soaring through skies, with a purpose divine.

Each beat of its wings, a song of the past,
Embracing the fire, its shadows amassed.
A blazing rebirth, in the night's tender hold,
The cycle of life, both brilliant and bold.

Through ashes and smoke, it takes to the air,
A spirit unbroken, stronger for care.
With each lofty rise, it embraces the dream,
Unfolding the tales woven tight at the seam.

The world below watches, in awe of the sight,
As the phoenix ascends, igniting the night.
With vibrant resolve, it brightens the gloom,
Whispering stories of life from the tomb.

So heed the call of the heavens on high,
For the phoenix dreams as it journeys the sky.
In the realm of the timeless, rebirth finds its way,
And life dances on in the light of the day.

## Twilight Song of Rebirth

In the twilight's embrace, where day turns to night,
Soft melodies linger, a whisper of light.
The stars begin twinkling, a tale to unfold,
Of dreams reborn in shades of soft gold.

With shadows entwined in the dusk's gentle breath,
The essence of life dances close to sweet death.
Yet from the deep silence, new hopes will arise,
Painting the canvas of infinite skies.

As the world holds its breath, waiting for dawn,
Every heartbeat echoes the magic to spawn.
In the gentle twilight, all sorrows find peace,
And the song of rebirth whispers sweet release.

Beneath the pale moonlight, a promise is spun,
That after each darkness, new journeys begun.
In the cradle of starlight, the quiet dreams play,
Woven together, to light up the way.

So gather your wishes, let them take flight,
In the twilight's soft hue, find your heart's own light.
For every sweet ending holds something more bright,
In the song of rebirth, all will feel right.

## Resurgent Echoes of Ashes

In the silence that follows the fire,
Whispers of dreams rise like smoke,
Fragile hopes, a heart's choir,
Yearning for light, no longer a cloak.

From the embers, new lives take flight,
Reviving the past in a radiant dawn,
Each echo a promise, burning bright,
Transforming the grief into a song.

The shadows of yesterday fade,
As phoenixes stretch wings anew,
Through remnants of sorrow, we wade,
Finding strength in the ashes we rue.

Time spins a web with each breath,
Woven tales of loss and of gain,
In a cycle of life, love, and death,
Resurgent echoes break every chain.

So let the embers guide our way,
Toward horizons kissed by the sun,
In the dance of the dusk and the day,
From ashes to beauty, we run.

## The Woven Path of Fire

Beneath the stars, a path unfolds,
Threads of flame and shadows bright,
Each step a story, a tale retold,
A tapestry spun in the moonlight.

The flickering flames of fate align,
Casting visions of dreams to chase,
With every heartbeat, a sacred sign,
A journey woven in time and space.

Through trials fierce, we walk the line,
Embracing the heat of the unknown,
In the forge of struggle, we entwine,
A tale of courage that we've sown.

As fire dances in the dark,
Let passion guide where spirits soar,
In every spark resides a mark,
Of the woven path we can explore.

Together we rise, through pain anew,
With hearts ignited, forever bright,
Bound by the flames that show us true,
On the woven path, our souls ignite.

## **Wings of Iridescent Desires**

In twilight's glow, a dream takes flight,
Wings adorned, in colors unfold,
Chasing the stars, beyond the night,
The essence of wishes, daring and bold.

A whisper of hope flutters near,
Echoing longings, sweet and clear,
In gentle breezes, we shed our fear,
As iridescent wings draw us near.

With every heartbeat, visions gleam,
Casting shadows on the worlds we know,
Embracing futures, more than a dream,
In each shimmering moment, we grow.

Together we rise, unbound by fate,
Carried by winds of unseen tides,
In the dance of the cosmos, we await,
For desires to soar where love abides.

With wings of light, let hearts conspire,
To touch the skies, to find our song,
In realms of wonder, we'll never tire,
With iridescent dreams, we belong.

## Dancing Through the Flames

In the heart of the fire, we sway,
Embracing the warmth that lights our skin,
Each flicker a rhythm, guiding our way,
As shadows and flames begin to spin.

With laughter and tears, we join the fray,
A dance of resilience in the night,
Through trials fierce, we won't delay,
Finding freedom in fire's bright light.

In the crackle of wood, our spirits rise,
Unfurling like banners that kiss the sky,
Each step as bold as the stars' surprise,
In this tempest of passion, we fly.

Together we whirl, lost in the heat,
A symphony played on the edges of fate,
With every heartbeat, our souls repeat,
In dancing through flames, love won't wait.

So let the fire ignite our dreams,
With every twirl, a story we weave,
In the glow of the night, laughter beams,
Dancing through flames, we find what we believe.

## **The Resilient Tangle**

In the heart of the thicket, trees intertwine,
Roots stretch like fingers, grasping for the divine.
Whispers of secrets in the rustling leaves,
Tales of the timeless, the air gently weaves.

Amidst tangled branches, a spirit takes flight,
Dancing through shadows, embracing the light.
Wounds of the past begin to mend slow,
Hope like a river, in the depths it will grow.

Nature, the teacher, shows strength through despair,
In storms we are forged, in trials we lay bare.
Each throb of the earth echoes courage anew,
Resilient as ever, life breaks through the blue.

With blossoms of promise, the future unfolds,
Stories of wonders in every heart told.
Entangled we stand, united and free,
The resilient tangle of you and of me.

Together we flourish, each root intertwines,
Finding our way through the old dark confines.
In the dance of the wild, we reclaim our grace,
The cycle of seasons, a steady embrace.

## Wings Whispering New Beginnings

Beneath the soft glimmer of dawn's tender glow,
Wings spread in silence, with hopes set to flow.
The air heavy laced with the scent of rebirth,
A promise of changes wafts over the earth.

Birds in the treetops, a symphonic tune,
Each note lifts the spirit, beneath a bright moon.
With courage like feathers, we dare to ascend,
In flight we discover what lies 'round the bend.

On winds of adventure, our hearts take the lead,
Embracing the unknown, planting each seed.
With whispers of freedom, the journey does call,
Wings whispering softly, with no fear of the fall.

Through valleys of shadows and mountains so steep,
We gather our dreams like stars we can't keep.
In sunrise reflections, each soul learns to soar,
Wings whispering wisdom, forever explore.

As dawn turns to day, the horizon awakes,
New beginnings glitter like shimmering lakes.
With hearts wide open, we'll fly on the breeze,
Wings whispering softly, a sweet life to seize.

## Shadows of the Burning Dawn

In the hush of the morning, where shadows entwine,
The sun peeks with caution, the stars still align.
A dance of the worlds as night yields to day,
In whispers of twilight, lost dreams drift away.

With flickers of colors that paint the dark sky,
Echoes of secrets that never ask why.
Shadows of stories from the night's gentle hold,
Reveal hidden wonders, the brave and the bold.

Through mists that are shrouded in soft twilight's breath,
We ponder the truths found in moments of death.
Yet embers of hope in the dawn's golden glow,
Ignite all our spirits, the path we must go.

In shadows we dwell, yet fear not their guise,
For dawn bears the promise, with brightening skies.
Each line carved in memory, cherished with time,
Shadows of the burning dawn help us to climb.

With hearts forged in fire, we stand hand in hand,
Finding courage in shadows that strengthen our stand.
Together we rise, as the day calls to start,
Shadows of the burning dawn ignite the heart.

# Ember Strands of Fate

In the flicker of twilight, where firelight plays,
Embers whisper softly, recalling old days.
Each spark a reminder of trials we face,
Woven in time, like a delicate lace.

Threads of our life spun in laughter and tears,
The fabric of moments, the weave of our fears.
Amidst all the chaos, we find strength to cope,
Ember strands of fate weave a tapestry of hope.

Through shadows that linger, we gather our might,
In darkness, we shine through, illuminating the night.
With flickering brilliance, our voices unite,
Ember strands of fate lead us toward the light.

Found in the ashes of what used to be,
Rise stories of courage, setting our spirits free.
As fire ignites, and our hearts gently race,
Ember strands of fate shape our journey's embrace.

With the glow of tomorrow, we beckon the dawn,
Embracing the moments where dreams are reborn.
Bound together in spirit, our journey's not late,
In the warmth of connection, ember strands of fate.

## Phoenix Within a Radiant Mist

In twilight's glow, a feathered spark,
Emerges from the shadows dark.
With every rise, a whispered plea,
A heart reborn, wild and free.

Through silver fog, its flames ignite,
A dance of courage, pure delight.
With wings that shimmer, tales unfold,
Of bravery and dreams retold.

In the realm where wishes meet,
The phoenix soars, a rhythmic beat.
Through trials faced, it learns to fly,
In radiant mist, beneath the sky.

Nestled in warmth, the past gives way,
To vibrant colors of the day.
Each ember glows, a story scribed,
In fiery hues, the soul imbibed.

From ash to glory, life defined,
A testament to spirit, blind.
In every rise, a brand new quest,
The phoenix sings, its heart at rest.

## **Ashen Tales of Ascendancy**

Within the silence, shadows dwell,
In whispers soft, they weave their spell.
Amidst the ruins, stories bloom,
Of heroes lost and fate's own loom.

From ashes gray, a spark ignites,
Chasing the dusk, embracing lights.
Each tale told, a truth embraced,
In echoes past, our strength replaced.

Upon the winds, the voices rise,
Of every soul who dared to fly.
Through tempest's roar, and calm's defeat,
An epic forged beneath our feet.

Each ember glows, a heart's resolve,
In shadowed paths, we find, evolve.
The lessons learned through pain and strife,
Are woven deep into our life.

With every breath, a legacy,
A woven tapestry to see.
From ashen tales, we rise anew,
In every dawn, our dreams pursue.

# Fabric of the Celestial Wing

In starlit skies, the fabric gleams,
A tapestry of whispered dreams.
Each thread a story, sewn with care,
Unfolds the journey through the air.

With each beat of the winged flight,
The universe shines, pure and bright.
Celestial whispers, soft and clear,
Guide the lost souls, drawing near.

Through cosmic realms, they weave and swerve,
In dance of fate, the stars preserve.
Embracing light, they seek the dawn,
In shadows cast, their hope is drawn.

From nebula's heart to earthly ground,
The fabric pulses with a sound.
Each shimmer holds a story rare,
Of those who dared to truly care.

In harmony, they rise and spin,
The magic weaves, the tales begin.
Through every thread, our dreams take wing,
In fabric bright, life's song we sing.

## Flames That Narrate

In flickering light, the shadows dance,
Telling tales of fate and chance.
Each crackle holds a secret deep,
The flames that wake, the flames that leap.

Through ember paths, the stories flow,
Of love and loss in fire's glow.
Upon the hearth, the legends spark,
In vivid hues, igniting dark.

With every flicker, memories rise,
Unraveling truth through smoky sighs.
The fire speaks, its voice a guide,
In warmth and light, we cannot hide.

Past battles fought and victories earned,
In flames, the wisdom swiftly learned.
The dance of time, it weaves and twirls,
A tapestry of boys and girls.

Between the logs, a world unfolds,
In every whisper, history holds.
For flames that narrate, fiercely bright,
Reflect our lives in the depth of night.